SUCCEEDING
AS
A
Self-Directed
WORK TEAM

20 IMPORTANT QUESTIONS ANSWERED

If you don't already have them—you'll want to know how they're revolutionizing the workplace. Why they're producing unbelievable results in quality and productivity in companies that use them.

If you already have SDWTs, you'll want to learn how to maximize the results and make yours the very best!

You'll want to read this before your competition does!

Succeeding As A Self-Directed Work Team

by Bob and Ann Harper

Printed and bound in the United States of America

Library of Congress Catalog Card Number: 90-91983
ISBN 1-880859-00-9

A partial list of companies that have purchased
Succeeding As A Self-Directed Work Team

Allstate, Inc.	GE Company	Ohio Bell Telephone Co.
American Express	GE Canada	Olin Chemicals
AT&T	Gate City Steel	PA Blue Shield
Becton Dickinson	General Motors	PepsiCola
Bridgestone	Goodyear	Petro Canada
C&P Telephone	Hallmark Cards	Pilgrim Health Care
CAMCO	Harris Corp.	Pillsbury Co.
Carrier Corp.	Hewlett-Packard Co.	PPG Industries
Champion Int'l.	Honeywell	PSE&G
Ciba-Geigy	Hyde Tools	Puritan-Bennett
Cigna Corp.	Hylsa Steel-Mexico	R.R. Donnelley & Sons
Cincinnati Milacron	IBM	Reynolds Metals Co.
COMPAQ	Indianpolis Life Ins.	Rochester Telephone
Coors Brewing	Intel Corp.	SPX Corp.
Cottonwood Hospital	James River Corp.	Scott Paper
Digital Equipment	Johnson & Johnson	Sears & Roebuck
Dover Elevator	Lear Siegler Corp.	TRW
E.I. Dupont	Lukens Steel	TVA
East Valley Camelback	Miller Brewing Co.	Texas Instruments
Hospital	Moen, Inc.	Textron
Eaton Corp.	Monsanto	Thomson Electronics
Emerson Electric	National Car Rental	The Timken Company
Employers Reinsurance	New York Life	Trane Co.
Ernst & Young	Insurance Co.	University of North Texas
Exxon	Northern Telecom	University of South Carolina
Fisher Controls	Norton Company	U.S. West
Food Lion Inc.	Ocean Spray	US Postal Service
GECC	Cranberries Inc.	Xerox

Our Purpose

This book was written to provide information first, then thought-provoking questions for you, the reader, to answer. These questions are designed to help you think through and clarify for yourself some of the most important issues surrounding SELF-DIRECTED WORK TEAMS and the dramatic changes they bring about. These questions can also serve as the basis for some interesting discussions with your entire team.

It is our hope that this book will provide Managers, Supervisors, Team Leaders and, most especially, Team Members, with useful information. And, equally as important, inspire you to have faith that this is the right direction to go and that SDWTs will work if teams are given the right training and support.

It's high time democracy came to the workplace. We must maximize the brains, talents and hard work of everyone at work if we are to survive as an economy. Better decisions, better ideas, etc. and constant improvement will produce the world-class quality and service we have to have. The only real question is: how fast can we do it?

About The Authors

BOB HARPER, PRESIDENT, MW CORPORATION, has worked with major companies for more than 20 years. He has worked for the GE Company, General Motors and IC Industries. In 1983 Bob formed MW Corporation, a full service consulting firm whose guiding belief is that training and development when it's designed and delivered well, taps the unlimited potential of human beings. Unlike machines, human beings never need to become obsolete. On the contrary, people are the greatest resource any company has. Bob has been preaching the principles of employee-involvement, participation for years! He is optimistic that, finally, people are listening.

ANN HARPER, ASSOCIATE, MW CORPORATION, has taught and written about SDWTs for the past five years. Helping companies transition to this new way of working has been very exciting and personally satisfying. Ann has participated in the design and development of public workshops and custom-designed programs in the areas of: Management Development, Supervision, Team Leadership, Team Development, Motivation, Active Listening, Change and Transition, Sales, Quality Customer Service and Self-Directed Work Teams. Ann is married to Bob and they often work together. They live in Westchester, a suburb of New York City.

Table of Contents

Question 1:
Is This A New Idea?

Self-Directed Work Teams have produced impressive improvements in quality, productivity, and customer service in both manufacturing and service industries.

The idea of a self-directed workforce is old and new. Experiments in this concept have been around for more than twenty years. SDWTs are a continuation of Quality Circles and other worker participation programs that have proven successful in Japan and in the U.S.

What's new about the idea is the seemingly strong commitment behind SDWTs today on the part of American management who have traditionally resisted employee involvement programs even though they produced results because this meant making changes management was not comfortable with. Several companies have now publicly committed them-

1

selves to this concept and many others are already experimenting at a rapid rate. (Specific examples listed under "Question 5: Do they work? What's the evidence?" pp. 19-26.)

What's driving the movement for SDWTs are several trends that we think are going to affect every American worker (if they haven't already):

1. **UNPRECEDENTED CHANGE:** Nothing is stable and predictable anymore in American business, so flexible, empowered (able to do what is right) workers are the only kind that can respond to a customer in a timely manner.

2. **COMPETING WITH A GLOBAL WORKFORCE:** Since goods can be made anywhere, American workers are competing with workers all over the world to prove that they can produce the highest quality goods and services at the lowest price.

3. **CONSTANT IMPROVEMENT:** Quality is defined by the customer and standards keep increasing so every worker's ideas, suggestions, and innovations are needed.

4. **LIFETIME LEARNING:** Skills for a lifetime are gone. Every worker will have to train and retrain constantly to stay ahead of the competition.

5. **WORK REDESIGN:** How work is produced will have to constantly be reexamined to make sure the best, "smartest" way of working is

found. Team based production for the making of goods and delivery of service will also be part of work redesign.

6. **INFORMATION TECHNOLOGY:** Everyone in an organization can now send and receive information directly. Computers, fax machines and other new products enable all workers to act on good, reliable information that has traditionally been given only to managers.

7. **SPEED:** Not only do we need to constantly respond to customers, deliver high quality at lower costs, and introduce new products, but we need to do all this quickly—before we lose customers to a competitor who is more nimble than we are.

8. **OPPORTUNITY:** It is a time of unprecedented opportunity for people who are flexible and companies who can remove the barriers that kill off good ideas.

This is an important moment in history—and if you are part of a self-directed workforce, you're participating in shaping the future of American business. Your success will save your job, your company, and possibly change the entire system of relationships between—worker-manager-union-company, that we have had for the past 200 years!

4

QUESTIONS FOR YOU:

When did my organization first begin thinking about SDWTs?

_____

_____

_____

_____

_____

If you already have SDWTs, when did they first begin?

_____

_____

_____

_____

_____

What trends are having an impact on your particular job, organization, etc.?

_____

_____

_____

_____

_____

_____

_____

Are SDWTs an attempt to address these trends?

_____

_____

_____

_____

_____

_____

_____

_____

Question 2: *What Is A Self-Directed Work Team?*

This concept goes by many different names: Self-Directed Work Teams, Self-Managing Teams, High-Involvement Workforce, etc. The teams themselves vary depending on what makes sense to the work of the organization. A general definition, therefore, is a group of employees (anywhere from 5-15 on the average) who are responsible for a whole product or process. The team plans the work and performs it, managing many of the things supervision or management used to do.

The team meets regularly (once a week or every day) to identify, analyze, and solve problems. They may schedule, set goals, give performance feedback, hire, fire, etc. The team's duties grow with their skills. They aren't expected to do all these things at the beginning; their responsibilities are increased as their new skills are mastered and the team grows and develops.

SDWTs vary depending on what makes sense to the type of work being performed, but generally, they share the following characteristics:

- Members possess a variety of technical skills. (They have been trained to be multi-skilled and able to perform each other's jobs.)

- They are accountable for production, quality, costs and schedules (in some teams members interview and hire new people, do appraisals, make repairs, monitor statistical process control, coordinate with other departments, etc.).

- Members have (with the help of training) interpersonal skills that teamwork requires (communication, feedback, problem-solving, decision-making, etc.).

- The team is constantly encouraged to increase skills, improve the product or service, solve problems, etc.

QUESTIONS FOR YOU:

What is my organization calling the teams?

_____

_____

_____

_____

_____

How is my organization defining a SDWT? (Size, job duties, skills, etc.)

_____

_____

_____

_____

_____

_____

_____

Question 3:
How Is It Different From Traditional Work?

1. Teams of multi-skilled employees are responsible for doing a whole job (an entire piece of work, not just a task) and accountable for producing specified end results.

2. Quality control and maintenance are part of the team's responsibilities not separate functions.

3. The teams schedule which members will do a task; some assign rotating tasks.

4. Leadership is shared; not performed by a supervisor (if there is a designated Team or Group

Leader, he/she is more of a facilitator supporting the group as coach and trainer rather than the traditional "boss").

5. Customer satisfaction and business goals are the focus, therefore SDWTs need information and feedback on quantity, quality, scheduling, cost, etc. In other words, information traditionally reserved for management is supplied directly to the team so it can establish goals and monitor progress.

6. SDWTs meet regularly (some daily, some weekly) to solve problems and in this way be self-correcting. Team meetings are spent:

   • Diagnosing, analyzing, and solving complex problems.

   • Reviewing workloads, giving work assignments, reviewing performance, etc.

7. Members receive training in: technical skills, interpersonal skills, team skills, etc.

8. SDWT members develop trust, candor and caring for each other.

9. People are paid for skills and productivity not just time.

10. A "can do" attitude that grows out of commitment, involvement and having a say is at the heart of the philosophical difference.

QUESTIONS FOR YOU:

How is this (or how is this going to be) different from my old job?

_____

_____

_____

_____

_____

_____

How do I feel right now about this change?

_____

_____

_____

_____

_____

_____

What do I see as the pluses and the minuses of SDWTs over traditional work?

_____

_____

14

Question 4:
Why SDWTs Now?

Experiments with SDWTs have taken place in American industry since the late 1950s. It has only been in the last decade that global competition has brought about a drive to dramatically increase worker participation, commitment and brain power in the workplace. The cause that is driving this change is usually QUALITY. The realization has been that money does not buy quality; people create quality. Automation helps, but committed people and smart systems are the key ingredients. Supervisors and managers can spot quality problems, but only workers can prevent problems from occurring.

Another cause has been CUSTOMER SERVICE. Only highly-skilled, committed, empowered (able to do the right things) workers can be flexible enough to quickly respond to ever-changing customer needs.

To put it bluntly: Organizations are realizing that their survival depends on the commitment and skills of their workers. The SDWT is a new way of viewing the relationship of the worker—management—organization. During the last decade no significant quality or productivity improvement in major organizations has been possible without worker involvement and commitment.

The success stories have all had at their core giving workers more information, more decision-making, more control over their work, more involvement, more ownership—out of this has come more commitment to end results; and more satisfaction for the worker.

Work teams are more committed and more responsive to the ever-changing global marketplace. Work teams can constantly improve the system by keeping data, solving problems and staying ahead of the competition.

QUESTIONS FOR YOU:

What is the compelling reason we are moving to SDWTs now or thinking about doing this now?

_____

_____

Have the compelling reasons (the "Why are we doing this?")
been clearly communicated to everyone?

_____

_____

_____

_____

_____

_____

Do I agree or disagree with the reasons?

_____

_____

_____

_____

_____

_____

_____

Question 5:
Do SDWTs Work?
What's The Evidence?

According to data from the Work in America Institute, the following companies use work teams:

Procter & Gamble since 1962
Cummins Engine since 1973
General Motors since 1975
Digital Equipment since 1982
Ford since 1982
Tektronix since 1983
LTV Steel since 1985
GE Company since 1985
Caterpillar since 1986
Champion International since 1986
A. O. Smith since 1987
Boeing since 1987

Xerox, Blue Cross, Harley-Davidson, Westinghouse, Logan Aluminum, Rohm & Haas, Shenendoah Life, Honeywell, Motorola, Johnsonville Sausage, Aid Association for Lutherans, the U.S. Postal Service and the Philadelphia Zoo are just some of the organizations, large and small, that are currently experimenting with work teams.

SOME SPECIFIC EXAMPLES:

- Monsanto Company has achieved quality and productivity improvements 47% higher than four years ago. Part of the changes at Monsanto involve giving workers more freedom and participation through the use of work teams. "I knew 20 years ago I could direct my own job, but no one wanted to hear what I had to say," says a team leader of mechanics who divide the work and make key decisions as a team with no foreman. (Business Week, August 1989)

- Logan Aluminum in Russelville, Kentucky, reduced turnover by 20% in just 2 years and reduced absenteeism to 1.2%.

- Rohm & Haas Bayport, Inc. in LaPorte, Texas, has for more than 5 years had all 67 employees of the plant (4 teams) play an active role in managing the plant (no shift foremen or supervisors). Turnover rates have gone from 50% to less than 10%. Rohm and Haas has expanded this concept to other plants in Bristol, PA, Houston, TX, Knoxville, TN, and Louisville, KY.

- GE Ohio Lamp Plant in Warren, Ohio, began about a year ago redesigning the entire workplace

(750 employees) into teams. In an extraordinarily cooperative partnership, union and management are now reducing job classifications from more than 100 to less than 20.

- GE National Customer Service Center for Lighting in Richmond, Virginia, is a greenfield operation set-up about a year ago to take the place of 25 separate order centers. Everyone (even clerical people) are part of a team. The center manager meets with every team once a month to listen to them.

- A. O. Smith Corporation in Milwaukee, Wisconsin, is a 100 years old auto components company that has proven the team concept can be put into operation in a traditional factory or office. Working with seven different unions, A. O. Smith learned to manage jointly with the union and has started restructuring its production system.

- At Quad Graphics (high-quality magazine printers) there are only two layers of management between the CEO and the teams that do everything: hire, fire and have responsibility for almost everything. There is no purchasing or personnel department; this is all done on the shop floor where printers deal directly with customers. The guiding principle is trusting people to be responsible professionals and constantly training everyone. People even train a 1/2 day a week on their own time after they have finished their 12 hours, 3 days a week workload. Employees own 40% of the company and see their growth and the company's as unlimited.

- At GM's Delco-Remy plant in Fitzgerald, Georgia, the average SDWT member does all maintenance and repairs on machines, keeps track of his/her own time, handles all housekeeping, is responsible for safety, has access to a lock-free tool room, advises on new equipment purchases, recruits new team members, does budget preparation and review, participates in ongoing problem-solving activities, rotates as team leader, and is paid for knowledge (continuous learning). The plant consists of 25 operating teams and several technical service teams who all report to a support team made up of the plant manager and direct reports. The teams are responsible for all quality control.

- In 1985 a shuttered General Motors factory in California reopened as a joint venture with Toyota Motors Corporation. The NUMMI assembly plant is now hailed as proof that a labor and management success story can be created in American heavy industry. Union leaders and management are proud of the success achieved by the teams. A bigger say in how they performed their jobs, resulted in satisfied, more productive employees. Both sides have pointed to NUMMI as proof that with the right organizational system, American factories could take on anybody in the world. In terms of productivity, NUMMI products are ranked no. 2 on quality surveys (no other GM car even appears on the list of the top 15).

The average NUMMI team consists of 4-8 people with one member as a team leader paid 50 cents more an hour. The team leader handles administrative duties, fills in for absent workers, and helps those having trouble finishing their work. When sales of the Chevy Nova slumped in 1988, production was cut but no workers were laid-off. Instead, workers received training in problem-solving and interpersonal skills and helped prepare another assembly line for new models.

There is presently no profit-sharing plan. Rewards are given for suggestions that improve efficiency but no system to share the financial gains of higher productivity.

Recently several union members have criticized NUMMI for too much pressure on workers, replacing supervision with peer pressure, inhumane absentee practices, etc. But when MIT interviewed the workers themselves, none of them wanted to go back to the old way. All agreed the work was hard but they also felt NUMMI offered a better chance for survival than the traditional adversarial relationship between labor and management that previously existed in the plant that closed.

Under the Japanese Management at NUMMI, there are no special parking or dining privileges. Senior executives and workers all wear the same uniform, park in the same lots, and eat in the same cafeteria.

On both sides of the assembly line, cords hang within easy reach of workers. Every worker has the "right and obligation" to pull the cord and stop the line to prevent defective cars from continuing down the line. If a worker falls behind or cannot finish his/her operations, he/she pulls the cord and team leaders and group leaders converge on the problem. The line shuts down until the problem is fixed. NUMMI executives say the ability of ordinary workers to stop the line symbolizes the relationship of trust between labor and management.

A big issue is the pace of work. Management pushes to get the most out of workers. If one team is constantly pulling the cord, some of their work is shifted to another team or more labor is added. The system also rotates workers through all the jobs a team must perform, so the workload is balanced and tedium minimized. NUMMI workers get involved in designing their own jobs in collaboration with their team and group leaders, but management decides how much work a team is assigned. Teams are also expected to constantly refine their methods to save time.

NUMMI is the first Japanese managed auto plant in the U.S. with a UAW workforce paid union wages and benefits. In just four years it has achieved quality and productivity levels exceeding anything in the U.S. and rivaling the best Japanese plants. Its success is attributed to its revolutionary team production system.

- Johnsonville Foods in Sheboygan, Wisconsin, is a company where 500 employees take lifelong, continuous learning seriously. The typical work team here:
  - Recruits, hires, evaluates and fires.
  - Trains for new skills constantly.
  - Works on its own budget.
  - Handles all quality control, inspection and problem-solving.
  - Suggests new product ideas.
  - And more.

The firm has grown to more than $100 million, since adopting its new approach to the workforce about six years ago.

- Aid Association for Lutherans in 1987 created 16 multi-functional self-managed teams. The objective was to destroy 12 functions and rigid job descriptions and in so doing speed and improve the insurance products and service offered. Employees are paid for knowledge and cross-trained. The company believes fewer employees with upgraded skills can do more in less time.

- Harley-Davidson in York, Pennsylvania, has in just 6 years returned to profitability and successfully competes with the Japanese by creating work teams. This new attitude is summed up by a Harley line worker, "It's our motorcycles, whether we have a title or not."

- Honeywell, Xerox, Motorola, Ford, General Motors and Westinghouse have all committed to using a more participative way of managing people. And they are not just talking about a few plants, but the entire organization.

- According to a recent article in Business Week (July 10, 1989) 20% of GE's workforce of 120,000 U.S. employees now work under the team concept and the corporate goal is to have 35% of the workforce in teams by the end of 1989. According to Robert Erskine, a manager of production resources, "We're trying to radically reduce the work cycle needed to produce a product...when you combine automation with new systems and work teams, you get a 40% to 50% improvement in productivity."

- AT & T Credit Corp. in 1986 set up 11 teams of 10-15 newly hired workers processing lease applications. Three major functions were combined in each self-managing team with members deciding how to best deal with customers, schedule their own time off, reassign work during absence and hire new team members. Seven regional managers provide the only management and advise team members rather than telling them what to do and how to do it. The results: teams process up to twice as many lease applications as they did under the old system and approvals can be done in 1 to 2 days vs. the several it used to take (Business Week, 1989).

- John Hopkins Hospital, Maryland, developed a nursing team model that gives nurses greater autonomy and pays them a salary, not an hourly wage. The 12 teams in place, so far, have reduced turnover, cut absenteeism, and a surgical unit team reports a 21% increase in patient volume. The nurses' decide by consensus whether or not to adopt this model. John Hopkins is hoping all of its nurses reorganize in the next 3-5 years.

The evidence that SDWTs work is compelling and every day more and more companies are experimenting with some form of employee involvement. Yet, most experts feel we are still moving too slowly. We still need management, labor and unions to form the kind of partnerships needed in order to radically improve our quality, productivity, service and employee job satisfaction.

QUESTIONS FOR YOU:

Which examples of companies or divisions using SDWTs have I heard about?

_____

_____

_____

_____

_____

_____

_____

Which sites have I visited?

_____

_____

_____

_____

_____

_____

What do I think about what I'm hearing or seeing firsthand?

_____

_____

_____

Question 6:
What Are The Key Elements Of High-Performing Teams?

Research on High-Performing Teams indicates the presence of the following key elements:

1. The team understands the goals and is committed to achieving them. There is a lot of participation by everyone, but if the discussion strays from the subject, someone brings it back. There is a lot of discussion of the task and how to best accomplish it. Everyone feels a high degree of involvement in formulating tasks and commitment to accomplishing them.

30

2. The team creates a climate where people are comfortable and informal. Trust replaces fear and people are able to take risks. It is a growth and learning climate where people are involved and interested.

3. Communication is open and honest among team members. People feel free to express their thoughts, feelings, ideas, etc. Members listen to each other and everyone feels free to put forth an idea without being criticized. Conflict and disagreement are considered natural and dealt with. The emphasis is on resolution not personalities.

4. Team members have a strong sense of belonging to the group and commitment to its actions. There is a sense of being included, of being part of the team and a sense of pride in its accomplishments.

5. Team members are viewed as unique people with valuable resources. Diversity of opinions and ideas are encouraged rather than "Groupthink." Flexibility and sensitivity to others is practiced.

6. Creativity and risk-taking are encouraged.

7. The team is able to constantly improve itself as a team by examining its processes and practices. The team looks periodically at what may be interfering with its operations. Open discussion attempts to find the causes of problems whether they are procedures, individual behavior, etc. and develop solutions instead of letting problems worsen.

8. The team develops procedures to diagnose, analyze and solve problems.

9. Participative leadership is practiced (whether the group has an appointed leader or leadership shifts among the members). The leader does not dominate the group. Different members, depending on their particular knowledge or experience, lead the group when their expertise is called for. Everyone is used as a resource.

10. Members of the team make decisions together that are of a high-quality and have the acceptance and support of the members to carry them out.

QUESTIONS FOR YOU:

What was the best team experience I've ever had (in or out of the work setting)?

What made the team so effective?

32

_____

_____

_____

_____

How was it different from other teams I've experienced?

_____

_____

_____

_____

_____

_____

_____

Question 7:
Is This Effective For Every Workplace?

Philosophies on this question vary. Some experts believe the team should be the basic unit of any organization because all work is better carried out by a team of people who work together. Others believe the SDWT is best suited to people who do work that requires a segment of a final product or service, or a single product or service all the way through to completion. Support functions can also be performed by a work team—interviewing, training, maintenance, purchasing, etc. or these functions can be absorbed into the production work team itself.

Here are some examples of where SDWTs seem to work best:

- An insurance company work team is responsible for all phases of the customer service in a given geographic area—handling applications, processing claims and making payments. Formerly, each of these would have been performed by a separate group.

- A centrally located work team answers questions on employee benefits through an 800 number. Previous questions were answered by many more employees scattered throughout the company.

- An electronics assembly work team preps components, stuffs and solders them on printed circuit boards, tests and repairs boards, sets and monitors inventory levels, inspects, ships, receives and processes paperwork. Members are cross-trained in all the tasks.

- A work team assembles, paints and tests auto engines. Instead of an assembly line, the team uses a traveling stand which they wheel around as they add to the final product. They do not do any machining or purchasing at the front end of the process, or shipping and billing at the back end—yet.

- A centrally located order center for a lighting group takes orders by teams for geographic areas. Previously this work was performed by 25 different locations scattered throughout the country.

QUESTIONS FOR YOU:

Would more employee commitment and involvement improve the productivity, quality or customer service at my workplace?

_____

_____

_____

_____

_____

_____

Could a team of multi-skilled workers better produce our product or deliver our service (faster, more economically, etc.)?

_____

_____

_____

_____

_____

_____

Question 8:
What Are The Possible Drawbacks?

1. Management panics when production curves drop (as they often will during the early stages of work redesign) and support for the SDWTs weakens.

2. Teams do not receive the support they need:

   - goals are not clear

   - too little structure is provided

   - managers abdicate responsibility

   - team members are not trained in the skills they need to proceed

3. Democratic methods are alien to people accustomed to the more authoritarian methods of the past and so people need time to adjust. Some people do not like working this way and prefer the traditional way.

4. Leaders need to learn to gradually give over responsibility to teams. The refusal of some leaders to change roles—reverting back to the old way of doing things impedes the progress of the team's growth and development.

5. Since there is no one design that fits every workplace, each organization creates its own version. Reassuring people when you don't have all the answers is a very difficult leadership task and requires an act of faith on the part of the leader— faith that this will succeed despite very real obstacles.

6. Changes in leadership are a drawback when the new leader does not know how to lead in a SDWT system so he/she reverts back to traditional supervision.

7. When one pilot group is the experiment within other departments or divisions that are run in the old way—the maverick must have a strong commitment and management support from top to bottom in order to survive and grow. A good many pilots die out because of this peer pressure to conform.

8. Since this new way requires a lot of training and support, a problem can be moving too fast, before the necessary skills are learned.

9. In a union environment extraordinary cooperation is required throughout the process. Managers and union leaders must become partners in improving the workplace and this can only happen by letting go of traditional definitions and redefining what is possible in a win-win relationship.

10. When all the skills needed are learned, things could become routine. Introducing new products or systems is one answer to keeping teams fresh. Providing learning opportunities inside and outside the system is needed for renewing enthusiasm and challenge and constant improvement.

11. Additional skills and knowledge are needed, so training costs are increased.

12. Managers and supervisors may resist if they feel they will not be positively affected.

13. Expectations are raised by participative programs and if these are not met, the results will be frustration, disappointment, dissatisfaction and cynicism.

QUESTIONS FOR YOU:

Drawbacks or problems we are presently having?

_____

_____

_____

_____

_____

_____

_____

Drawbacks or problems I can see in the future?

_____

_____

_____

_____

_____

_____

What can we do about these problems?

_____

_____

_____

_____

_____

_____

What can I do?

_____

_____

_____

_____

_____

_____

_____

Question 9:
What Is Needed For Success?

In order to combat the drawbacks we just discussed, the following actions are needed:

1. MANAGEMENT SUPPORT. We mean by this commitment from top management that this is the right way to go and faith that given the time and resources, SDWTs will succeed.

2. PARTICIPATIVE LEADERSHIP. All managers need to understand and practice participation. They must relearn how to manage employees by sharing information, decision-making, rewards, and knowledge and involve people in everything. This is not easy since it requires turning the traditional pyramid upside down and turning the manager into a supporter, ad-

visor, coach, cheerleader, barrier-smasher, etc. Unless leaders change their behavior, SDWTs cannot succeed.

3. ELIMINATE TRADITIONAL SUPERVISION. The role of supervisor must change. The team needs a facilitator not a boss. Supervisors must be given new roles in the organization as their jobs are phased out. This requires assuring them that new roles (as team leaders, trainers, etc.) will be found or created for them. Without supervisors yielding their traditional control over things like scheduling, appraising, etc., nothing will change.

4. PATIENCE. 2-4 years is the general span of time it takes to develop a self-directed workforce, so patience and the ability to live with ambiguity is important. Usually the process begins with a steering committee who reads everything on the subject of SDWTs and visits locations so they can have some firsthand experience. Then, they appoint a design team to study the present system and recommend how it could be redesigned. After this, a pilot is begun.

5. TRAINING IN NEW ATTITUDES, NEW ROLES AND NEW SKILLS. For many organizations SDWTs mean adopting a new corporate culture of learning for everyone, all the time. The guiding belief is that there is no limit to what a trained, highly-motivated person can do.

6. UNION-MANAGEMENT PARTNERSHIP. New attitudes and definitions of the union-manage-

ment relationship must be mutually worked out. SDWTs cannot take place in an adversarial climate. Union and management must form a win-win partnership. The UAW is pushing ahead with employee involvement throughout the auto industry despite dissension within its own ranks because it believes this is the wave of the future if America is to stay in business.

7. EMPOWERMENT. SDWTs need the skills and the authority to achieve the quality, flexibility, responsiveness to customers, which give them the edge over traditional forms of work.

8. REWARDS. Reward systems must encourage SDWT members to learn the new skills, take risks, solve problems, give up traditional forms of security such as seniority, etc. Many companies are instituting some form of job security, pay for learning, profit-sharing, employee stock ownership, pay for productivity, etc.

9. ASSURANCES. Workers must be assured (through formal or informal means) that boosting productivity will not cost them their jobs. People cannot be expected to invent the means for eliminating their jobs unless they are assured that other, preferably better jobs are there for them.

10. MOTIVATION. Fear is not a motivator. Sometimes workers are told that they will become a self-directed workforce or the plant will close and they will be out of jobs. Threats like this (even if they are based on reality) will work only on a short term basis, if at all. Fear is not a motivator; it drives people down to the basic

46

security needs. People that are worrying about their jobs are not in the best state of mind to be productive and carry forth a work innovation as important and as challenging as Self-Directed Work Teams. Success in this area depends on providing people with real motivation—an inspiring reason to move forward. More challenge, better quality and productivity, more satisfying work (rewards, personal growth, etc.) are all reasons that compel people to change.

QUESTIONS FOR YOU:

Do we have management support?

How committed is this company to making SDWTs succeed?

_____

_____

_____

Are we being given the necessary support?

_____

_____

_____

_____

_____

_____

_____

Question 10:
What Are The Benefits For The Organization?

1. **MORE EFFICIENCY AND PRODUCTIVITY**

2. **HIGHER QUALITY**

3. **BETTER CUSTOMER SERVICE** - faster and more responsive

4. **WORKING SMARTER** - more able to do what's necessary to compete in global marketplace

5. **CONSTANT IMPROVEMENT** of the system and the process

6. **BETTER ABLE TO MAKE DECISIONS** that will keep the company ahead of the competition - **ABLE TO COMPETE IN TIME**

7. **UTILIZATION OF EVERYONE'S BRAINS, COMMITMENT, CREATIVITY,** etc.

8. **BETTER COMMUNICATION** up, down and sideways on what really matters

9. **WORLD-CLASS PRODUCTS** - the best company to deal with

10. **A MORE SATISFYING AND EFFECTIVE WORKPLACE** for all employees

11. **THE SENSE OF BELONGING AND COMMITMENT A TEAM BRINGS**

12. **CONSTANT GROWTH** for the organization through increasing its human resources - the people of the organization

---

QUESTIONS FOR YOU:

Benefits I can see or foresee for my organization?

Short-term?

———————————————

———————————————

———————————————

Long-term?

———————————————

———————————————

———————————————

———————————————

———————————————

———————————————

———————————————

Question 11:
What Are The Benefits For The Team Member?

1. **MORE INVOLVEMENT** in the decisions that affect one's work

2. **MORE PERSONAL PRIDE** in the quality of the product or service

3. **REWARDS** tied to productivity (money saved, problems solved, etc.)

4. **ABILITY TO SOLVE PROBLEMS**

5. **ABILITY TO INNOVATE CHANGE**

6. **A FEELING OF OWNERSHIP** in the company

7. **EMPOWERMENT** (able to do what is right and needed)

8. **INDIVIDUAL GROWTH AND DEVELOPMENT** - constant training and development of technical skills, interpersonal skills, team skills, etc.

9. Tapping into one's **LEADERSHIP ABILITIES**

10. **THE CAMARADERIE AND SUPPORT OF A TEAM EFFORT**

11. **VARIETY AND CHALLENGE**

12. **MORE INFORMATION, KNOWLEDGE AND DECISION-MAKING CAPABILITY**

QUESTIONS FOR YOU:

What are the benefits for me now?

_____

_____

_____

_____

_____

_____

_____

In the future?

_____

_____

_____

_____

_____

_____

_____

Question 12:
Can Anyone Learn To Be An Effective Team Member?

Most people enjoy working in teams, but not everyone. People are different, their needs are different, and what they like to do varies. But, provided a person enjoys working in teams and given the proper training, anyone can be an effective team member.

Over the years we've asked people to describe the characteristics of the most effective team they've ever been a part of. Some people describe teams at work, others teams in the military, sports teams, etc. but the characteristics of effective teams are all generally the same:

- The goals were clear.

- All the members were aiming for the same goal.

- Members knew each other and worked closely together.

- The team's achievement was higher than any member could have done alone (synergy).

- The achievements were higher than anyone expected.

- Members trusted each other.

- Working with the team was enjoyable.

- People listened to each other and were sensitive to each other's needs.

Most people derive heightened work satisfaction from the collaborative efforts of a team they're proud to be part of. SDWT members need training in the following areas in order to be effective:

- Interpersonal communication (disclosure and feedback)

- Stages of group development (knowing what to expect as a group developes)

- Conflict resolution

- Effective team meetings

- Problem-solving

- Decision-making

- Etc.

With the right support and training anyone who enjoys working in teams and is willing to learn and change can become an effective team member.

QUESTIONS FOR YOU:

Things I like about working in teams?

_____

_____

_____

_____

_____

_____

_____

Things I don't like about working in teams?

_____

_____

_____

_____

_____

What can I do to change the things I don't like?

Question 13:
How Is Leadership Handled By The SDWT?

Some SDWTs have no designated, permanent leader. Instead, leadership is shared by all the members. One person might be the leader when safety is the topic; someone else might lead if quality is being discussed. In this way the leadership is shared by the group members and shifts depending on the specialty under discussion.

In other "leaderless" groups the specialty area shifts after several months. So that first I'm the leader in quality as I learn statistical quality control and then I become the leader for safety and receive training in that area while someone else becomes leader in quality.

Other SDWTs have a designated, permanent leader usually called a Team or Group Leader. This is a member of the team who is paid extra for also leading the group and representing the group to a Coordinator who is responsible for several teams.

Whoever leads the group must be skilled in being able to facilitate the group in reaching decisions and solving problems, not dictate to the group what it needs to do. If SDWTs are to be effective, they must have an environment where everyone, but especially the leader:

1. Makes sure everyone has a say.

2. Listens to everyone.

3. Believes everyone is a resource.

4. Sees to it that everyone grows and develops.

5. Understands that everyone has different needs and sees to it that everyone is motivated.

6. Sees to it that synergy is achieved. (Synergy: the total is more than the sum of the parts or team results are better than any one individual effort.)

7. Values diversity (the uniqueness of people).

8. Attacks the problem, not the person.

9. Doesn't suppress conflict, but handles it effectively.

10. Creates a climate of trust and open communication.

11. Encourages everyone to learn and take risks.

12. Rewards achievement.

13. Supports through coaching, counseling, and advising.

QUESTIONS FOR YOU:

How has our team decided to fill the leadership role?

_____

_____

_____

_____

_____

_____

_____

Would I like to lead or share leadership of a SDWT? Why or why not?

_____

_____

_____

Question 14:
What Is The "New Role" Of Manager And Supervisor?

In order for any employee involvement innovations to take place, Managers and Supervisors must change the way they have traditionally led employees. This is very difficult because we have developed these leaders in traditional settings and habits are hard to change, but not impossible. Those leaders that have successfully made the transition have found it to be exciting and personally satisfying and so worth the initial frustration, confusion, etc.

The job of changing is doubly difficult because our organizations are becoming leaner (less managers) and the very idea of a Self-Directed Work Team means the Supervisor will eventually be replaced by the group. Therefore, it is the task of the organization to make Managers and Supervisors feel that though their jobs are changing, they, as people, are still valuable (perhaps more than ever) and their expertise will be needed in other ways (training, support functions, team leadership, etc.)

In order to facilitate this new way of operating, Managers and Supervisors will need to:

1. Become skilled in empowering—turning over power, information, knowledge, skills, decisions, to others.

2. Become skilled teachers and counselors—excited by other people learning and growing.

3. See their jobs as almost totally people-oriented.

4. See themselves as facilitators of frontline people rather than decision-makers and rule enforcers.

5. Spend a good deal of their time removing barriers across functions that hinder frontline people; eliminating excessive procedures.

6. Become skilled at listening to people vs. telling people what to do.

7. Become skilled at asking what can we do differently and better.

8. Be able to solve problems on the spot instead of just passing them up or down.

9. Be a good role model as a leader—modeling the behavior they want others to do.

10. Be a visible leader—one who is available to people.

11. Be open, honest and worthy of trust.

12. Do the right things.

13. Stop killing the messenger and see some mistakes as necessary learning.

14. Encourage risk-taking.

15. Love change. See it as opportunity.

16. Become customer & employee-driven.

17. Be a motivator.

18. Promote teamwork.

19. Believe there are no limits to the ability to contribute on the part of properly selected, trained, supported, committed and involved people.

20. Have faith in SDWTs as the right way to go even though you don't have all the answers.

21. Constantly learn.

68

22. Be flexible—open to new ideas and other ways of doing things.

23. Reinforce and reward the new behaviors.

24. Respect people.

25. Trust people.

26. Celebrate progress.

QUESTIONS FOR YOU:

What new behaviors on the part of Managers and Supervisors are needed in your organization?

What new behaviors have you seen already?

Question 15:
What Different Attitudes Are Required?

The "new" attitudes required in order to achieve successful SDWTs are exemplified by the following differences:

From:	To:
Technology first	People first
People as Spare Parts	People As Valuable Resources
Control-Supervisor	Commitment-Teams
Procedures Book	Self-Control

From:	To:
Many Levels	Flat Organization
Autocratic Style	Participative Style
Directive Decision-making (1 person decides)	Consensus Decision-making (The group decides)
Competitive	Cooperative
"Tell me what to do"	How can *we* work smarter?
"It's Only a Job"	"It's My Job"
Skilled in one job	Constantly learning
Low Risk-taking	Innovation
Reacting to change (Reactive)	Seizing opportunities (Proactive)
Stability & Predictability	Constant Change
"We'll think about it and set up a committee to study it"	Do it faster than the competition (compete in time)
Management & Union as Adversaries (Win-Lose)	Management & Union as Partners (Win-Win)
Internal Organization Driven	Customer-Driven
Rules Bound & Slow	Flexible & Fast
Doing Things Right	Doing the Right Things
"I only work here"	"I am the company"

From:	To:
Power over workers (Told what to do)	**Empowered workforce** (Able to do what is right)
If it's not broken, don't fix it	**Constant improvement**
Acceptable Quality & Service (Good enough)	**World-Class Quality and Service** (The Best)

QUESTIONS FOR YOU:

What attitudes of mine have I already changed?

_____

_____

_____

_____

_____

_____

_____

Which attitudes do I still have to work on changing?

_____

_____

_____

_____

_____

_____

_____

Which attitudes on this list (if any) do I just not agree with?

_____

_____

_____

_____

_____

_____

_____

Question 16
What New Technical Skills And Training Are Needed?

Learning is the key to Self-Directed Work Teams. As a member of a team you will have to learn two types of skills: Multiple Technical Skills and Multiple Team Skills.

The technical skills you will learn will depend on the nature of your job. In most work teams you will learn how to do the job of each member of your team. This will take quite a bit of time and training, but the advantages will make it worthwhile.

Here are just some of the many benefits of multiple technical skills:

1. Ability to fill-in for each other when a member of the team is absent.

2. Ability to help each other out during times when important work has to be completed on a deadline.

3. More effective problem-solving because everyone shares the needed information.

4. More empathy for the other guy's problems because you know his/her job and what they're up against.

5. More ability to be creative and innovative about the work because each of you has knowledge of each part of it.

6. More personal growth and career development for you because you are a multi-skilled worker and thus more valuable and marketable.

7. Less repetition means no boredom. Work becomes more interesting, challenging and satisfying.

8. Rewards and recognition from the organization for your hard work and good ideas. Some organizations have pay for learning systems and/or some form of profit-sharing where new learning and productivity are compensated.

9. Tracking skills (statistical process control, charts, diagrams, etc.) enable people to understand how the systems work and improve them without tam-

pering (making them worse). Since quality control and improvements will now be the responsibility of the team, tracking the cause of problems so they can be eliminated will be very important.

QUESTIONS FOR YOU:

What new skills will I have to learn right away?

_____

_____

_____

_____

_____

_____

_____

What new skills will I have to learn over time?

_____

_____

_____

_____

_____

_____

_____

How do I feel about learning these new skills?

_____

_____

_____

_____

_____

_____

_____

Question 17:
What Team Skills And Training Are Needed?

The Team Skills you'll need will also vary somewhat from organization to organization, but in general, these are the new skills that team members will need training in:

1. Team Development training in how to become an effective team member of a work team and what the characteristics are of effective teams (see "Key Elements of High Performing Teams" pp. 29-31).

2. Leadership training if your team has decided to have no formal leader and instead rotate the leadership among all the members.

3. Problem-solving skills to solve or begin to solve work problems.

4. Decision-making skills for making effective decisions that have both quality and group acceptance.

5. Interpersonal skills (communication, conflict resolution, presenting, listening, giving and receiving feedback, etc.) to better enhance the effectiveness of the team.

6. Administrative tasks traditionally performed by supervisors will now, most likely, be performed by the team. Team members need training in safety, hiring, firing, appraisal, etc. Members would gradually learn these skills and only take on the task after receiving the proper training.

7. Customer service training, especially if there will now be more direct interface with external or internal customers, vendors, etc.

8. Team meeting skills for effective, productive meetings.

QUESTIONS FOR YOU:

What new team skills will I need to learn right away?

_____

_____

_____

What new team skills will I need to learn eventually?

_____

_____

_____

_____

_____

_____

How do I feel about learning these new skills?

_____

_____

_____

_____

_____

_____

_____

Question 18:
How Do We Get Started?

Both start-ups and redesigns begin with a lot of reading, talking and visiting other sites to see how SDWTs really work. Workers, managers, technical people, etc. need to dialogue and look at the entire organization. A central question is: *Is there a problem or opportunity here that work redesign could address?*

A STEERING COMMITTEE is then appointed made up of top management, union officials (if there is a union), and other key people (workers, engineers, supervisors, managers, team leaders, etc.) The steering committee discusses the philosophy and values this new system will embody and how things will be different from the traditional workplace. Team building for this group is helpful in order for people to feel open and honest with each other's thoughts and feelings concerning this new venture. Visiting other companies together also builds rapport. A consultant can be helpful in facilitating the process.

The Steering Committee then chooses one or more design teams to look at the entire present system and suggest ways it can be redesigned to optimize productivity. Members of the DESIGN TEAM should be representative of all levels and functions so that each part of the organization feels part of the process.

The Design Team usually consists of:

- Some members of the steering committee
- Key managers/supervisors/team leaders
- Key functional people with technical expertise
- Key union people
- Any others representing parts of the organization

Typically the Design Team does the following:

1. Looks at the needs of outside customers, vendors, the government, etc. who exert an external influence on the organization. The team examines how the organization is presently responding to these environmental demands.

2. Looks at how the present system works technically. The team studies how the entire system functions: how and where errors occur, raw materials needed, quality requirements, etc. and what needs to be redesigned.

3. Looks at how the present system works socially and how redesign could create: increased job satisfaction, job enrichment, job coordination,

cross-functional relationships, leadership and supporting roles, etc.

4. Examines every aspect of the current system: hiring, firing, training, planning, scheduling, compensating, repairing, etc. and looks for opportunities to improve these things in agreement with the new philosophy and values the new system will embody.

5. Spends time reading, taking courses, talking and listening to people, visiting other companies that are already working this way, etc.

6. Gives periodic presentations to other groups on the status of their findings and receives valuable feedback on various work design proposals under consideration. Everyone's involvement here is important. People who actually do the work need to say how feasible the new design is. Free and open discussions are crucial to getting everyone's involvement and ultimately, everyone's commitment to the new design.

7. Prepares a design and implementation proposal. Three months is about the average time a design team takes to get to this point. This plan is discussed with all affected parties before it is approved by the steering committee.

8. Usually a pilot group is then chosen either by asking for a group of volunteers who want to do this or by picking a group because they meet certain criteria and would have the best chance of succeeding. Then, other teams are added gradually.

Important Considerations:

1. *Each organization has to create an original design that uniquely fits their workplace.* It has to make sense to everyone and take into account what is best for the process and the people.

2. This process of designing better work for everyone has worked in new sites and redesigns of traditional factories and offices (with union and non-union workforces).

3. Fragmented jobs are turned into whole tasks that a team completes for its customers.

4. The aim is for everyone to understand how the whole system works and to be empowered to act on behalf of a customer.

5. Action-orientation is the goal. High-quality decisions can be made swiftly by teams of highly committed workers who are empowered to do what is right.

6. Everybody's job will change. Some designs include a responsibility chart which shows how the team will, over time, take over the tasks performed by staff and supervision. This transition period helps everyone receive training and gradually adjust to new roles in the organization.

7. This process of establishing this new way of working usually takes a minimum of 2-3 years in order for gains in productivity, quality and job satisfaction to take effect.

8. This is a very exciting and frustrating time. Not everyone can work in this new environment and options should be available to everyone.

QUESTIONS FOR YOU:

Is your organization a start-up or a redesign?

_____

_____

_____

_____

_____

_____

Have a steering committee, design team and pilot group been chosen or do you already have several SDWTs?

_____

_____

_____

_____

_____

_____

How would you assess progress thus far? (moving too fast, too slow, just right, etc.)

_____

_____

_____

_____

_____

_____

_____

If you have a pilot team, what has been the reaction to it?

_____

_____

_____

_____

_____

_____

What has been a success thus far?

_____

_____

_____

_____

_____

_____

_____

What has been a problem?

_____

_____

_____

_____

_____

_____

_____

Is there a transition plan in place?

_____

_____

_____

_____

_____

_____

What is the general reaction to all this change on the part of the average worker?

_____

88

...The average supervisor?

...The average manager?

Question 19:
What Stages Does A SDWT Go Through And What To Do At Each Stage?

Effective SDWTs develop over time; they cannot be produced instantly. Experience has shown that a period of 2-3 years is required in order for effective SDWTs to develop in an organization. Before high-performance, full efficiency and satisfaction is achieved, certain predictable stages evolve.

Although the particulars would vary depending on the people and the organizations, the following 3 Stages are generally expected:

STAGE I:
Since no one knows quite what to expect there is a lot of confusion, uncertainty and frustration in the beginning. There can also be a lot of excitement on the part of some people, but not everyone. Roles are changing, people are learning new skills and learning is frustrating (remember learning to ride a bike for the first time).

The people who have the easiest time during Stage I are those that have faith in the philosophy of SDWTs and are personally committed to making them succeed. These are the people who look for the small successes even at this early stage and who communicate the little victories, who praise the heroes, etc. They don't look for the failures (which are inevitable) and they don't find reasons for why it will never work.

Getting through Stage I requires a focus on learning, an ability to tolerate mistakes and deal with frustration, and faith that SDWTs will succeed here as they have elsewhere. Reading about and visiting successful sites can help.

STAGE II:
During this stage the teams are becoming united. Members have a sense of belonging. If there are designated team leaders, there is usually a reliance on them to guide the team and keep it together. The wise leader understands this and slowly gives up the control to the team because only in this way will the team grow to its full capability. Decisions made by the leader must slowly be given over to the team. The team is learning to trust itself during this stage and good decisions, problems solved, etc. should be recognized and rewarded by the organization. A lot of training is taking place at this time. Measurement enables team

members to track their progress. More teams are usually added at this phase.

STAGE III:

At this final stage most of the multiple technical skills and team skills training has taken place. The team is effective in carrying out both its task duties (the work itself) and maintenance duties (growing the team). The team members feel ownership of the team and the work, responsibility for solving problems, and have knowledge of how the whole system works. They also feel they can significantly impact that system.

At this point tying rewards to productivity (pay for learning, profit sharing, etc.) makes sense. The SDWT is now world-class competitive, working on continuous improvement of everything. Quality and customer service should now show significant improvement over previous work systems. And members should also feel more satisfaction than ever before. But since there is no end to learning, the team continually strives for improving the work and the satisfaction of individual members.

EVOLVING THROUGH EACH STAGE:

The changes we've been describing are dramatic and we as human beings do not take well to change. We like our habits and cling to them even though we know we shouldn't. So, at each stage of change, certain questions need to be answered, again and again, so these new behaviors are reinforced. Some of these important questions are:

Why are we doing this? What is the compelling, driving reason for all this change?

_____

_____

_____

_____

_____

_____

_____

Is it important that we do this? What might happen if we don't?

_____

_____

_____

_____

_____

_____

_____

Is this doable?

_____

_____

_____

_____

_____

_____

_____

What am I supposed to do? (What are my goals, objectives, etc.)

_____

_____

_____

_____

_____

_____

_____

How am I doing? (Is there feedback provided to me on how well I'm doing or what mistakes I'm making?)

_____

_____

_____

_____

_____

_____

_____

_____

How will I benefit? How will we benefit?

_____

_____

_____

_____

Is there support available?

_____

_____

_____

_____

_____

_____

What happens if I make a mistake?

_____

_____

_____

_____

_____

_____

What are we going to be like when the change has taken place? (Is the vision, mission clear to people?)

Who cares if we succeed? (Does this really matter to people?)

If you are in a leadership role, you will need to answer these questions constantly, and if you're not, you will need to seek out the answers to these questions and answer them for yourself. If we have a clear idea of how we want to change, a personal plan for achieving the goal, and a clear idea of the benefits that we'll gain when we get to the other side, we'll

have a much better chance of succeeding at anything
we undertake.

Question 20:
What Else Can I Read About SDWTs?

Goodman, Paul S. *Designing Effective Workgroups.* San Francisco: Jossey-Bass, 1986.

Hackman, J. R. and G. R. Oldham. *Work Redesign.* Reading, MA: Addisson-Wesley, 1980.

Harper, R. L. and A. L. Harper. *Skill-Building for Self-Directed Team Members: A Complete Course.* New York: MW Corporation, 1992.

Hess, Karen, editor. *Creating the High Performance Team.* New York: John Wiley & Sons, 1987.

Lawler, E. E. *High Involvement Management.* San Francisco: Jossey-Bass, Inc., 1986.

Likert, Rensis. *New Patterns of Management.*
New York: McGraw-Hill, 1961.

Nora, John J., C. Raymond Rogers & Robert J. Stramy.
Transforming the Workplace. New Jersey: Princeton
Research Press, 1986.

Peters, Tom. *Thriving on Chaos: Handbook for a Management Revolution.* New York: Alfred A. Knopf, 1987.

Schonberger, Richard J. *World Class Manufacturing Casebook: Implementing JIT and TQC.* New York: The Free Press, 1987.

Waterman, Robert H. *The Renewal Factor.*
New York: Bantam Books, 1988.

Weisbord, Marvin R. *Productive Workplaces: Organizing & Managing for Dignity, Meaning & Community.*
San Francisco: Jossey-Bass, 1987.

A Final Note:

SELF-DIRECTED WORK TEAMS work! The evidence is all around us that when you involve employees in managing their own work and correcting problems that stand between their pride in producing a quality product, the results are higher productivity, higher quality and greater satisfaction.

Yet, the American business community has been reluctant to adopt genuine employee involvement. Witness what has happened to Quality Circles—successful in Japan while dying a slow death here. It is sadly ironic that our American management principles were successfully exported to Japan by Americans like W. Edwards Deming and others, while American companies failed to adopt these ideas. When they clearly worked in Japan, American management gave the credit to Japanese workers. Now the Japanese plants in America have proven that employee involvement works here with American workers. So there are no excuses left, only the facts: American management has to change if we are to compete in the 1990s and beyond.

Self-Directed Work Teams can work if leadership at the top is committed to the primary idea that everyone in the workplace is valuable, everyone is a resource, and everyone is capable of constantly learning to improve themselves, their work and the organization.

Workplaces who involve their people in improving something every day for a customer, will thrive and flourish.

We Would Like To Hear From You:

Call or write to us to let us know how you used this book:

1. What information did you find particularly helpful?

2. What, if anything, would you like to see included in future reprints?

3. What ideas on SDWTs have you formed from your experience that might be useful to other people?

4. What books, articles, other resources have you found helpful?

5. Would you like to be part of a network of people who are presently involved in or thinking about SDWTs? Would you be available to call or visit as a resource?

6. Would you like the names of other people you could use as a resource?

Call (914) 528-0888 or write to MW Corporation, 3150 Lexington Avenue, Mohegan Lake, New York 10547. Ask for Ann or Bob Harper.

TO ORDER ADDITIONAL COPIES AND FIND OUT ABOUT OTHER PRODUCTS (BOOKS & VIDEOS) CONTACT:

MW Corporation
3150 Lexington Ave.
Mohegan Lake, NY 10547

or Call: (914) 528-0888
or FAX: (914) 528-8889

SUPPORT SERVICES:

MW Corporation offers a full-range of support services for making your Self-Directed Work Teams successful:

Consulting Services, Presentations, Public Workshops and Custom-Designed On-Site Training and Development for:
• Steering Committees
• Design Teams
• Team Leaders/Facilitators/Coordinators
• Managers
• Work Team Members

Please call 914-528-0888 for a free COURSE CATALOG describing our public workshops (with dates and locations) and customized on-site training in management and team development, leadership, active listening, continuous improvement, customer service and other key areas for organizations and individuals in the '90s.

Notes

Notes

Notes